D0429234

Cover photograph by Carlos E. Santa Maria/Shutterstock. Photographs throughout the book are from: Getty Images, Shutterstock Images, Jupiterimages Unlimited, iStockphoto, and PhotoSpin. Photographs on pages 39 and 128, courtesy The Church of Jesus Christ of Latter-day Saints. Photograph on page 55, John Bytheway. Photograph on page 75, McKay Christensen. Photograph on page 86, Wally Joyner.

Library of Congress Cataloging-in-Publication Data

Bytheway, John, 1962-
  Sports : life lessons from court, field, and gridiron / John Bytheway.
     p. cm.
  Includes bibliographical references.
  ISBN 978-1-60641-092-9 (hardbound : alk. paper)
  1. Sports—Religious aspects—Church of Jesus Christ of Latter-day Saints.
  2. Conduct of life. I. Title.
  GV706.42.B98 2009
  796.01—dc22   2008053669

Printed in China
R. R. Donnelley, Shenzhen, China

10   9   8   7   6   5   4   3   2   1

SPORTS

Life Lessons from Court, Field, and Gridiron

JOHN BYTHEWAY

DESERET
BOOK

SALT LAKE CITY, UTAH

ACKNOWLEDGMENTS

Thanks to Chris Schoebinger, my product director, for his encouragement; Emily Watts for her wonderful editing skills; and Shauna Gibby for the beautiful design. Thanks always to Sheri Dew and Deseret Book for sticking with me over the years.

What counts in sports is not the victory, but the magnificence of the struggle.

JOE PATERNO
Long-time football coach of Penn State

66 Sports can develop the body in strength and endurance. They can train the spirit to meet difficulties and defeats and successes, teach selflessness and understanding, and develop good sportsmanship and tolerance in participant and spectator. 99

PRESIDENT SPENCER W. KIMBALL

PRE-GAME

Who invented sports? It all began in 1841 in a small log cabin in Rupert, Illinois, where Samuel H. Sports sat daydreaming on a Saturday afternoon. While surveying the hardwood floor, his eyes came upon a sizable ball of yarn beneath the rocking chair. Looking upward, he spied a circular hole in the roof of similar size. Inspired, he leaned over, picked up the ball of yarn, looked up at the roof and threw it towards the hole. . . . (I'm sorry, I just made that up.)

So where did sports really come from? One interesting theory is that sports were a by-product of the industrial revolution. There was a time when mankind had to hunt in order to eat. The skills of running, chasing, calculating speed and distance, throwing things, and hitting targets were necessary in order to survive. Then the industrial revolution hit, and over time, many men moved into factories and others into large-scale farming. Machinery and technology provided food.

In the meantime, what could be done with the accumulated skills of running, chasing, throwing things, and hitting targets that mankind had developed over the centuries? Answer? Sports. With the exception of golf, most major sports were invented *after* the industrial revolution.

Although the average man doesn't use them very often, hunting skills are still held in high regard. In fact, centuries later, we still respect—no, that's not strong enough—we still revere—no, that doesn't quite say it either—we *worship* the skills of running,

chasing, throwing things, and hitting targets to the point that we leave our homes on Saturday afternoons, pack our bodies with thousands of others into stadiums and gymnasiums, and sit for hours and hours to watch others use these skills. It used to be that we ate wild game and shot at targets. Now we watch wild games and shop at Target.

But wait—it gets even more interesting. We begin to identify with a group of athletes who have honed these skills, and we thrill to see them run, chase, throw, and hit targets in competition with another group of athletes. If our group doesn't hit as many targets as we had hoped, it ruins our whole weekend. If our group excels, we feel we have won a victory ourselves, and we taunt our

brother-in-law and our co-workers who chose another group to follow. Strange stuff, these sports.

Why do we love sports so much? Perhaps it's because a basketball, baseball, or football game is like a miniature lifetime—an unscripted, unpredictable drama where determination, adversity, persistence, exhilaration, and disappointment are all acted out in front of us culminating with either the "thrill of victory" or the "agony of defeat." Spectators who watch the game become part of the drama themselves, and that's part of the thrill.

After four quarters or nine innings, these contests are over. But there are lessons to be learned there that can be applied to the faceless opponents we confront in everyday living. Life comes at a slower pace than sports, but how we play this "game" of life is infinitely more important.

As a teacher, I am constantly looking for life lessons in everyday things, and I can find plenty of them in sports. In this book, we'll

talk mostly about basketball, baseball, and football. We'll look at the observations of coaches, players, and even Church leaders concerning sports.

Now that the pre-game chat is over, it's time for the tip-off, time to throw out the first pitch and kick off this little book, *Sports: Life Lessons from Court, Field, and Gridiron.*

BASKETBALL

I would venture to say that basketball is a part of Latter-day Saint culture, at least in North America. How many meeting-houses have you seen that *didn't* have a basketball court? I rest my case. Of course, we often call it the "cultural hall," but we all know what it is—a place for basketball on Saturday mornings, and a place for inexpensive wedding receptions on Saturday nights. ("Just camouflage the hoops, honey, and it will look just like a reception center.")

The only broken bone I've ever had was the result of a ward basketball game. Ward basketball helps LDS men learn to ask for forgiveness. I can't tell you how many stake priesthood meeting talks I've heard that began with a sheepish apology for behavior on the basketball court. I suppose that's a good thing. I'd probably

have to apologize too, since I know I've allowed my competitive spirit to get the best of me. When you've played together, perspired together, struggled together, and built a bond on the basketball court, perhaps it's easier to work together on service projects or your home teaching.

❝I am sure that no man can derive more pleasure from money or power than I do from seeing a pair of basketball goals in some out of the way place—deep in the Wisconsin woods an old barrel hoop nailed to a tree, or a weather-beaten shed on the Mexican border with a rusty iron hoop nailed to one end.**❞**

DR. JAMES NAISMITH
Inventor of basketball, the first real game of which was played in 1891

13

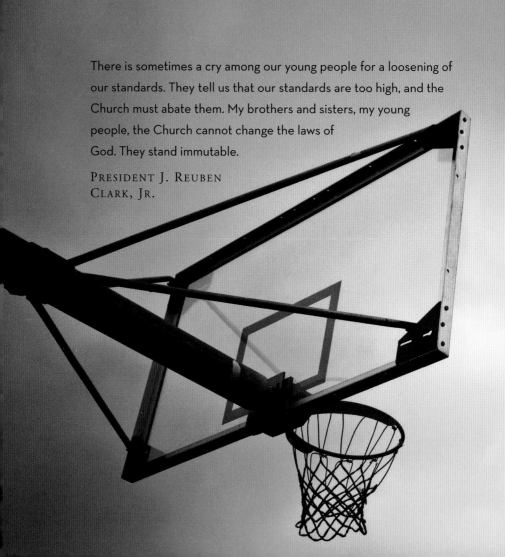

There is sometimes a cry among our young people for a loosening of our standards. They tell us that our standards are too high, and the Church must abate them. My brothers and sisters, my young people, the Church cannot change the laws of God. They stand immutable.

PRESIDENT J. REUBEN
CLARK, JR.

THE BASKETBALL "STANDARD"

Deacons shoot the ball to the same hoop the high priests do. That's the standard. If I were to come to your ward, or you were to come to mine and measure the distance between the floor and the rim, we'd both come up with the same answer—ten feet. That's the standard. In the game of basketball, we don't adjust the standard based on a player's height. High school, NCAA, or NBA, deacon or high priest, it's ten feet. We call them basketball *standards*, not basketball *variables*.

In the chapel, the bishop has a little switch to raise or lower the pulpit based on the height of the speaker. Imagine what it would be like if, in the NBA, the rim were raised or lowered each time a different player had the ball.

Similarly, we don't adjust the standards to accommodate our own weaknesses. Rather than changing the commandments, the gospel requires us to change ourselves, to adjust ourselves to the standard. That's one of the reasons I love basketball: whether you're five-foot-six or six-foot-five, the standard is ten feet.

PRACTICE MAKES PERFECT?

I remember practicing free throws at the stake center before a ward basketball game. I sank ten in a row and felt pretty good about myself.

During the game, I had an opportunity to demonstrate my skill. I clanked the first one, and the second rolled around, touching every inch of the rim before it finally fell through. I had always heard that "practice makes perfect," but in more recent years I've heard that idea challenged. "Practice doesn't make perfect," someone said, "practice makes *permanent*— only perfect practice makes perfect."

Reflecting later on my chance at the free-throw line, I remembered how winded I was at the time. My mouth was dry, my heart was pounding, and I was physically spent. Next time I practice free throws, I should do so after ten minutes of wind sprints to try to duplicate what it might feel like during a game.

Similarly, it's pretty easy to come up with the right answers and make good choices during Sunday School or priesthood meeting. But actually making those decisions when you're out in the world is another thing. The more we actually practice the gospel, the more we choose the right when wrong is staring us in the face, the more our spiritual muscles will grow and the better we'll be able to face adversity and temptation the next time they come around.

We Want Monson!

*S*omeone has said that courage is not the absence of fear but the mastery of it. At times, courage is needed to rise from failure, to strive again.

As a young teenager, I participated in a Church basketball game. When the outcome was in doubt, the coach sent me onto the playing floor right after the second half began. I took an inbounds pass, dribbled the ball toward the key, and let the shot fly. Just as the ball left my fingertips, I realized why the opposing guards did not attempt to stop my drive: I was shooting for the wrong basket! I offered a silent prayer:

"Please, Father, don't let that ball go in." The ball rimmed the hoop and fell out.

From the bleachers came the call: "We want Monson, we want Monson, we want Monson—out!" The coach obliged.

Many years later, as a member of the Council of the Twelve, I joined other General Authorities in visiting a newly completed chapel where, as an experiment, we were trying out a tightly woven carpet on the gymnasium floor.

While several of us were examining the floor, Bishop J. Richard Clarke, who was then in the Presiding Bishopric, suddenly threw the basketball to me with a challenge: "I don't believe you can hit the basket, standing where you are!"

I was some distance behind what is now the professional three-point line. I had never made such a basket in my entire life. Elder Mark E. Petersen of the Twelve called out to the others, "I think he can!"

My thoughts returned to my embarrassment of years before, shooting toward the wrong basket. Nevertheless, I aimed and let that ball fly. Through the net it went!

Throwing the ball in my direction, Bishop Clarke once more issued the challenge: "I know you can't do that again!"

Elder Petersen spoke up, "Of course, he can!"

The words of the poet echoed in my heart:

"Lead us, O lead us,

Great Molder of men,

Out of the shadow

To strive once again."

I shot the ball. It soared toward the basket and went right through.

That ended the inspection visit.

At lunchtime Elder Petersen said to me, "You know, you could have been a starter in the NBA."

PRESIDENT THOMAS S. MONSON

IT IS BETTER TO TRY SOMETHING GREAT AND FAIL, THAN TO TRY NOTHING GREAT AND SUCCEED

Sheri Dew played high school basketball, but wasn't sure if she was good enough to play in college. Later, as a student at BYU, she peeked into the gym where the BYU women's basketball tryouts were taking place. "Suddenly," she relates, "every insecure cell in my body began to scream, 'What are you thinking? You aren't good enough to play ball here! You can't compete with these girls! What has gotten into your head!'"

She never entered the gym, never tried out, and never knew if she could have made the team. Many years later, as Sister Dew related this story to a group of female athletes at BYU, Elaine

Michaelis pointed out that she was the basketball coach during that very time. She said: "In all my years of coaching, it is the *only* year I was not able to fill my roster, and we played that season one player short. All season I kept searching for one more girl to fill out our team, but I could never find her."

Sister Dew responded, "Ugh! When she said those words, it felt as though she had sucker-punched me. I couldn't believe it was true, but Elaine later assured me that it was. She had looked all season long for another player to add to her roster, but she had never been able to find that one particular ballplayer."

Sheri Dew had the courage to share that story so that more of us might have the courage to try.

In my coaching I informed every player who came under my supervision that the outcome of a game was simply a by-product of the effort we made to prepare. They understood our destination was a successful journey—namely, total, complete, and detailed preparation. Too often we neglect our journey in our eagerness or anxiety about reaching the goal.

JOHN WOODEN
Legendary basketball coach

*. . . If ye are prepared
ye shall not fear.*

D&C 38:30

"BE PREPARED"

As a young man, I had a fairly easy time memorizing the Scout motto. It's pretty short. The older I get, the more I see the wisdom in those two little words.

How does a basketball player deal with "performance anxiety"? How does he get the confidence he needs when the team is counting on him to make the shot, especially when thousands of fans are taunting and screaming and telling him he can't?

The only thing I can think of is *preparation*.

When I lifted a little Cessna 152 off the runway on my first solo, the thought came to me, "I've got to land this thing." But I also remembered that I had already done forty-five takeoffs and landings with an instructor. I had practiced and I was prepared, so the fear was under control.

I attended Highland High School with Mike Maxwell, who later played basketball at BYU. After Mike's freshman year, when Coach Frank Arnold bid the athletes good-bye in the spring, he asked the players to prepare for the next season. More specifically, he asked them to make—not just take—but *make* 25,000 shots that summer.

When Mike reported back for his sophomore year, he hadn't just reached Coach Arnold's goal. He had exceeded it—times four. Mike had shot, and *made*, 100,000 baskets. That's 200,000 points, most of them from the fifteen-to-twenty-five-foot range.

Now, what do you suppose would go through Mike's mind in a real game as the clock wound down and he was expected to take—and make—the shot? Would it be fear, because he had sat around all off-season? Or would it be confidence, along with the calming thought, "I've prepared for this moment more than a hundred thousand times."

Take our basketball program at the University of Kentucky: We see ourselves as the hardest-working team in America. That is our standard, the yardstick by which we measure ourselves. We try to live up to it every day. Are we the hardest-working team in America? Who knows? And who cares. The important thing is we believe it. That's our edge. In close games, when the pressure intensifies and the margin between who wins and who loses can be as thin as an eggshell, we believe that all our hard work, all the long hours, and all the perspiration will enable us to come out on top. Why? Because we deserve it. We deserve our victory; we feel we've sweated more blood than our opponents and will earn it the old-fashioned way.

RICK PITINO
Coach of the 1996 NCAA national championship team

Guess Who Said This?

"I have special luck with my shots tonight, the ball goes through the hoop again and again, and the game ends with our high school team the victors against the college team. I am the smallest player and the youngest on the team. I have piled up the most points through the efforts of the whole team in protecting me and feeding the ball to me. I am on the shoulders of the big fellows of the Academy. They are parading me around the hall to my consternation and embarrassment. I like basketball. I would rather play this game than eat."

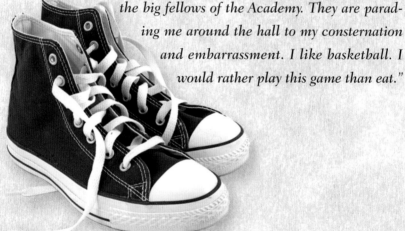

The player who wrote the paragraph on the left is pictured here on the far right—Spencer W. Kimball.

"JUST ME AND THE BASKET"

Basketball is a team sport, but individuals are center stage when they approach the free-throw line. At that moment, the arena is either silent or roaring, depending on whether the team is at home or away.

It seems to me that the pros always follow a set routine, for example: bounce the ball three times, look at the basket, flex the knees, spring, and shoot. Many players talk to themselves. Karl Malone of the Utah Jazz always seemed to be mouthing words to himself. Jeff Hornacek always touched his face with his hand while looking at the hoop. "Just me and the basket" is the phrase many players use to shut out all the noise and focus their concentration on what they need to do.

In life, we do not have home-court advantage. We're far from home. When peer pressure roars, when we're weakened by temptation and the whole world seems to be screaming at us to do something we don't want to do, we can come up with a phrase similar to "just me and the basket." Perhaps "choose the right," or "just do it," or one of my favorites in the face of peer pressure, "am I a warrior or a sheep?"

IT AIN'T OVER
'TIL IT'S OVER...

One of the interesting characteristics of a basketball game is you can be down by ten points with sixty seconds left in the game and still come back and win. Even if your team has been down the whole game, a three-pointer, followed by a steal and another three, and you're right back in it. Suddenly, it's a "two-possession game," as they say.

In basketball, scores can change so quickly that it doesn't much matter how you're doing in the first three quarters, or even late in the fourth quarter, as long as you're close. What matters is how you're doing right down to the double zeroes on the clock.

Basketball teaches that we must endure to the end. You can be true and faithful for many years and still mess up today.

Finishing strong in sports is important, but finishing strong in life can affect you forever. Paul finished strong, and expressed it like this:

"I have fought a good fight, I have finished my course, I have kept the faith: Henceforth there is laid up for me a crown of righteousness, which the Lord, the righteous judge, shall give me at that day: and not to me only, but unto all them also that love his appearing" (2 Timothy 4:7–8).

BASKETBALL IS A
TEAM SPORT

It's been a long time now, but I remember back in 1998 when the Utah Jazz swept the Los Angeles Lakers in the playoffs. I won't pretend to be an expert on why that all happened, but I do remember a comment someone made on the radio about the series. They observed that one team played like a "team of all stars," while the other played like an "all-star team."

Basketball players are not all alike, they certainly don't look all alike, but they don't have to—when they are united on a common goal. They can accomplish amazing things, as different as they are, when they work as a team. As someone once said, "Harmony is being different, together."

Let me use an example close at hand. I think of two young men who are both fine BYU basketball players. More important, they are both fine young men. But they are not alike in physical makeup or personal interests or academic majors or a hundred and one other differences that one person has from another. But we applaud that and understand it. Wouldn't it be foolish, even destructive, if these two men spent a lot of time wishing they were the other person? It would not help our basketball fortunes to have a nearly seven-foot man bringing the ball down the court nor one slightly over six feet playing the post position. Obviously, each of these young men has a task of his own, best suited to himself, and individual talents to develop.

If that is so obvious on the basketball court, why can't it be a little more obvious in life? Why do we allow ourselves to waste such energy and emotion comparing ourselves to others when our real task is to develop what we are and what we have, to be all that we can be?

PRESIDENT HOWARD W. HUNTER

BASEBALL

Baseball evolved out of several different "bat and ball" games, such as English Rounders, Cricket, and American Town Ball, which had been around for centuries. But there is one man who deserves the credit for establishing the fundamental rules of the sport and for organizing the first baseball game. He is Alexander Cartwright.

Cartwright was a member of the New York Knickerbockers, a club of young businessmen who regularly played Town Ball to escape the confines of their office lives and get some exercise after

work. In 1845, Cartwright and a commit-
tee from his club drew up clear rules
designed to convert Town Ball into a
more elaborate sport. He called it Base
Ball.

WHAT WOULD I DO IF THE BALL CAME TO ME?

One summer afternoon I was playing left field on the lower diamond at Lindsey Gardens, waiting for the next batter to come to the plate. I was a bit distracted, swatting a little swarm of gnats with my mitt, when my Little League coach left the dugout and shouted the word "think!" to the outfielders. That was his reminder to us to ask ourselves the question, *What would I do if the ball came to me?* (Eleven-year-olds need that kind of reminder sometimes.)

I quickly assessed the situation: No outs, one runner on second base; if the ball comes to me, I'll check the runner and throw to third base. If I catch it on the fly, I'll check to see if the runner remembers to tag up, then I'll throw to either second or third, depending on where he is.

The author in his Little League uniform

The pitcher wound up, threw the ball over the plate, and "CRACK!" the batter connected with the pitch. The ball took flight—it was a line drive—and it was coming right to me! It looked a little short, so I began to run forward, and although I was focused on the ball, I was surprised to see the runner advancing to third base. He didn't tag up! I caught the ball on the fly, took one step, and winged it over to the second baseman for a double play. "Nice job, Bytheway!" shouted Coach Duran from the dugout. *Phew. Thanks for reminding me to think!* I thought to myself as I returned to my spot.

I learned that day that it's better to "think first" than "think fast." I knew exactly what to do before it actually happened, so I didn't have to think it over. I already had a plan. My decision was already made.

Someday, if it hasn't happened already, temptation will come at you like a line drive. You'll be offered beer at a party, or a peek at pornography. Think fast—what will you do? If you think it over first, you won't have to think fast, you'll already know what to do. It's true in baseball, and it's true in life—it's better to think first than think fast.

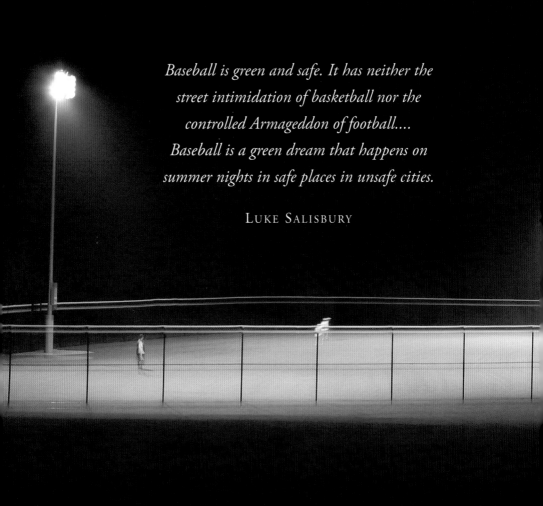

Baseball is green and safe. It has neither the street intimidation of basketball nor the controlled Armageddon of football.... Baseball is a green dream that happens on summer nights in safe places in unsafe cities.

LUKE SALISBURY

*L*ike some of you, I know what it is to face disappointment and youthful humiliation. As a boy, I played team softball in elementary and junior high school. Two captains were chosen, and then they, in turn, selected the players they desired on their respective teams. Of course, the best players were chosen first, then second, and third. To be selected fourth or fifth was not too bad, but to be chosen last and relegated to a remote position in the outfield was downright awful. I know; I was there.

How I hoped the ball would never be hit in my direction, for surely I would drop it, runners would score, and teammates would laugh.

As though it were just yesterday, I remember the very moment when all that changed in my life. The game started out as I have described: I was chosen last. I made my sorrowful way to the deep pocket of right field and watched as the other team filled the bases with runners. Two batters then went down on strikes. Suddenly, the next batter hit a mighty drive. I even heard him say, "This will be a home run." That was humiliating, since the ball was coming in my direction. Was it beyond my reach? I raced for the spot *where I thought the ball would drop, uttered a prayer while running, and stretched forth my cupped hands. I surprised myself. I caught the ball! My team won the game.*

This one experience bolstered my confidence, inspired my desire to practice, and led me from that last-to-be-chosen place to become a real contributor to the team.

PRESIDENT THOMAS S. MONSON

As we know, baseball has existed since the Creation.
Doesn't the Bible begin by saying, "In the big inning"?

No Fun without Fundamentals

When I was in a slump in the major leagues, one of the things my coaches would say was, "You're taking your eye off the ball; keep your eye on the ball!" Those basic fundamentals, no matter what level you are in the sport, need to be practiced again and again and again. I'm convinced that in our lives, in our occupations, on our missions, fundamentals are the key—the basic parts of the gospel that we need to make a part of our lives. As an athlete, fundamentals need to be second nature. It's not the flashy athlete that is successful over a long period of time. Sometimes it's not even the one with the most talent. I saw in my experiences in baseball, minor league players trying to get to the major leagues, some with a lot of talent, some with less talent. Those who

DALE MURPHY

worked consistently day in and day out on the fundamental things usually progressed faster than those with the talent that didn't work as hard.

DALE MURPHY

Murphy was the youngest player in Major League history to win MVP for two consecutive seasons. He was a seven-time All-Star and the winner of five Golden Glove awards. He was introduced to the gospel by another LDS player, Barry Bonnell.

"KEEP YOUR EYE ON THE BALL"

A s a Little Leaguer, I can't tell you how many times I was told to keep my eye on the ball. As a hitter, I was told to watch the ball all the way to the bat, and as an outfielder, I was told to watch the ball on the fly and to follow it all the way down into my mitt.

Today, when we hear about someone who made a mistake in some aspect of his or her life, it is often said, "He took his eye off the ball." The same principle is expressed in other ways—Stephen R. Covey has taught that "the main thing, is to keep the main thing the main thing." In other words, keep your eye on the ball! *Star Wars* fans will remember the X-Wing pilots being told by their commander as they approached the Death Star, "Stay on target,

stay on target." Focus and concentration in sports are vital, and focus and concentration in life are equally important.

As Latter-day Saints, our focus should be to seek the kingdom of God. If we do that first, all the rest will be added (see Matthew 6:33). If we don't seek the kingdom of God first, we've forgotten a major fundamental of life—we've taken our eye off the ball.

" I hope we will keep in mind and remember always the big ball game of life. We are all engaged in that game. Life is eternal. We are eternal beings. Softball is not the end. It is a means to the end. The end is the perfection of our Father's sons. The building of men of strength, men of character, and to do it joyfully, joyously, because He said that men are that they might have joy. **"**

"MY MISSION IS NOT FOR SALE"

I have half a dozen baseball cards at home. Not a huge collection, just a few I picked up while doing research for this book. One of my favorites is of McKay Christensen.

McKay was highly recruited for both baseball and football. As a high school running back, he held the California state record for touchdowns scored. Everybody wanted him for either sport, but McKay wanted to go on a mission. Something unprecedented happened. McKay was offered a million dollars to stay home and play Major League Baseball for the California Angels. A million dollars! McKay's answer was classic—"My mission is not for sale."

McKay was called to serve in Japan. While on his mission, he got up in the middle of the night to sign baseball cards, which was part of his contract. I have one of them. It says something on the back that you won't see on any other baseball card in the world:

> Christensen made a commitment prior to signing with California, therefore, he will begin his pro baseball career when he returns from his Mormon mission to Japan in 1996.

After his mission, McKay played for the Chicago White Sox, the Los Angeles Dodgers, and the New York Mets. To paraphrase 1 Samuel 2:30, "Those who honor God, God will honor."

MCKAY
CHRISTENSEN

 My motto was to always keep swinging.
Whether I was in a slump or feeling badly
or having trouble off the field, the only thing
to do was keep swinging. **"**

HANK AARON
Hall of Fame outfielder

GO DOWN SWINGING

A great life lesson from the game of baseball is caught in the phrase, "go down swinging." No baseball player is happy when he strikes out. But it's worse if he didn't even take a swing. You'll never hit any pitches you don't swing at. Stepping up to the plate and just hoping for a walk is a bad strategy. Looking for a good pitch and taking a swing is how you get a hit.

All of us will experience pain in life. But broken bones will heal, and most sicknesses will eventually give way to better health. Missed opportunities, however, will haunt you forever, so don't miss any! Even when we fail, we can find peace in remembering that we tried our best. But there's no peace in the memory that we didn't try our hardest.

To paraphrase Mother Teresa, "We are not called to be *success-ful* in all things, but to be *faithful* in all things." So we try. We try hard at every opportunity life gives us. If we go down, we go down swinging. We give it everything we have.

HARMON KILLEBREW

> 66 Harmon Killebrew could hit the ball out of any park in the country, including Yellowstone. 99

PAUL RICHARDS
Orioles manager

Latter-day Saint Harmon Killebrew hit 573 home runs in his career (currently #9 behind Mark McGwire for the top home-run hitters of all time). He was named an American League All-Star eleven times, and in 1984 was inducted to the National Baseball Hall of Fame.

Baseball is great. It is a good, clean, healthy sport, and millions of boys play and enjoy it. A few make it to the big leagues. Fewer still make it to the bronze plaques and statuary busts of halls of fame.

But all young priesthood men can make it to the greatest hall of fame there is, that of Eternal Life. This takes training, dedication, loyalty, integrity, and sacrifice; but more than any others the young men of the Church have the potential for it.

HARMON KILLEBREW

> ❝ Baseball is the only game left for people. To play basketball now, you have to be 7' 6". To play football you have to be the same width. ❞

BILL VEECK
Team owner

> ❝ If I dance after a home run, I don't think the pitchers would appreciate it. Baseball is a different game. In football, you're free to make a fool of yourself. ❞

DEION SANDERS
Two-sport athlete

> ❝ You can't sit on a lead and run a few plays into the line and just kill the clock. You've got to throw the ball over the plate and give the other man a chance. ❞

EARL WEAVER
Orioles manager

WALLY JOYNER

Luck Is When Preparation Meets Opportunity

My whole life people and players have come up to me and said, 'You're lucky. You've had a lot of opportunities come your way, and you're really lucky to be doing what you're doing and what you love to do.' Well, there's a saying that says, 'Luck is when preparation meets opportunity.' You have opportunities every day, and if you're not prepared for them, they're just going to pass you by."

WALLY JOYNER
Latter-day Saint All-Star baseball player

He's such a good, all-American kid.
You want to stand next to him in a rainstorm
because you know lightning won't hit him.

RON FAIRLY
Broadcaster, commenting on Wally Joyner

❝ The amazing contradictions in the game of baseball can be summed up in a feeling with which all players are familiar—even while standing on the mound with the ball in your hand and a lead on the scoreboard, you are struck by the stark realization that so much of the game is out of your control. Really, all you can control are your preparation, your effort, and your mental approach. . . . Isn't that how life is? We can't control anything beyond our preparation, effort, and outlook. The rest, including our destiny and how that destiny plays out, is in much bigger hands. **❞**

NOLAN RYAN

*Baseball is the very symbol, the outward
and visible expression of the drive and push
and rush and struggle of the raging, tearing,
booming nineteenth century.*

MARK TWAIN

> 66 This is a game to be savored, not gulped.
> There's time to discuss everything between
> pitches or between innings. 99

BILL VEECK
White Sox owner

> 66 You may glory in a team triumphant,
> but you fall in love with a team in defeat. 99

ROGER KAHN
Writer

> 66 May the sun never set on American baseball. 99

PRESIDENT HARRY TRUMAN

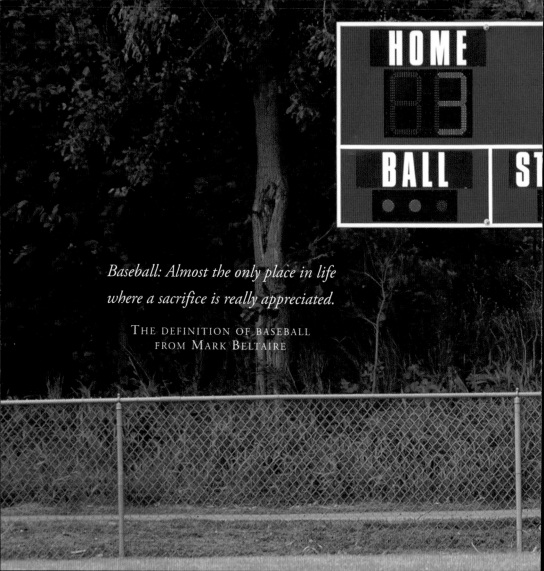

Baseball: Almost the only place in life where a sacrifice is really appreciated.

THE DEFINITION OF BASEBALL
FROM MARK BELTAIRE

THE SACRIFICE

What do the names Eddie Collins, Jake Daubert, John McInnis, Owen Bush, and Ray Chapman have in common? You say you've never heard those names before? They are all major league players with more than 300 sacrifice hits. In other words, they had the "opportunity" to bunt the ball or hit a pop fly and deliberately get out so that another player on their team could advance to the next base.

A "sacrifice," in baseball terms, wonderfully illustrates the team concept. I will give up a portion of my batting average, and the chance of hitting a single, a double, a triple, or a home run, for the good of the team.

Sacrifices in life always bring rewards when we're focusing on others. Many young men sacrifice two years of their lives to serve a mission, only to find that the rewards outweigh the sacrifice. Many parents sacrifice more profitable careers to focus on raising a family, but it seems the Lord always pays you back with interest.

Phillips Brooks observed, "How carefully most men creep into nameless graves, while now and again one or two forget themselves into immortality."

In football, the object is for the quarterback, otherwise known as the field general, to be on target with his aerial assault, riddling the defense by hitting his receivers with deadly accuracy in spite of the blitz, even if he has to use shotgun. With short bullet passes and long bombs, he marches his troops into enemy territory, balancing this aerial assault with a sustained ground attack that punches holes in the forward wall of the enemy's defensive line.

In baseball, the object is to go home! And to be safe! "I hope I'll be safe at home!"

GEORGE CARLIN

FOOTBALL

American Football (not to be confused with soccer, which is known as "football" by most people in the world) was invented by Walter Camp. The game traces its roots to rugby and soccer, the object being to get the ball to cross a goal line. Walter Camp introduced "line of scrimmage" and "down and distance" rules to give the game the character it has today. Later, the forward pass was added.

> ❝ Pro football is like nuclear warfare.
> There are no winners, only survivors. ❞
>
> **FRANK GIFFORD**

> ❝ You really don't want a president who is a football fan. Football combines the worst features of American life. It is violence punctuated by committee meetings." ❞
>
> **GEORGE F. WILL**

There are a lot of things that happen in a football game, or in the course of the season, that kind of mirror life. We have ups and downs, and adversities, discouragements, exhilaration, and you have to learn to keep all that in perspective. So I think those are some of the areas that a person playing the game can gain from it.

LAVELL EDWARDS

There is something to be said about young men acting with courage,
who fight as no one has ever seen young men fight before,
who have been taught by their parents and who hold true
to that, who perform with exactness.

BRONCO MENDENHALL

MY FOOTBALL RESUME

Football is my favorite team sport to watch and to play. When I was in grade school, every fall day, and I mean *every day*, I would meet with neighborhood friends and play football. On the grass? No, none of our yards were that big, and the closest parks were too far away. So we played on 4th Avenue—on the asphalt—between "L" and "M" street after school until it was dark. Occasionally we were interrupted by cars driving through our "field," if you can imagine the nerve of some people.

One time, while looking back for a pass, I ran into a parked Chevy Nova. I had always heard that bruises were "black and blue," but I got one on my thigh that day that included every color of the rainbow. It was cool. (The car survived undamaged.)

I didn't play high school ball—something about my neck size—but some of my greatest football memories are of playing intramural flag football as a student at BYU. Games were incredibly well-organized. They had referees, marked fields, and all you had to do was grab your elders quorum and show up. I wish those opportunities came up more often today. Now it seems all we do for exercise in elders quorum is help people move.

Although my experience is limited, I've had the thrill of catching a pass, throwing a touchdown, and running back a kickoff.

THE WILL TO PREPARE

> 66 My God-given talent is my ability to stick with training longer than anybody else. 99

HERSCHEL WALKER
Heisman Trophy winner and NFL running back

Perhaps more than the other sports mentioned in this book, football involves a disproportionate amount of preparation. Typically a team plays only one game per week.

Physical preparation, of course, is a year-round affair. Preparation for a game involves watching film on the other team, coming up with a game plan, and perfecting your own plays. Because of the nature of the clock in football, the portion of the game that involves the action between the referee's whistles is only about twelve minutes. Think about that—a week of preparation for *twelve minutes* of play time!

Life is like that too. I prepared for nineteen years to go on a mission for two. Every hour we spend sitting in the chapel is preparation for us to be strong in hard moments—the moments when we're not in the chapel, but out in the world of temptation. Preparation is the antidote for fear, worry, and nervousness—in sports as well as in life.

I talk about the importance of being prepared anytime I have the chance. To me, preparation is what success always hinges on. Emotion doesn't get you very far, and neither does a lot of talk. But preparation does. If you prepare yourself for whatever opportunities might present themselves during the season, then you're going to be successful. It's the players who work hard during the off-season (lifting weights and running and practicing their position skills) who find themselves in the middle of success once the season gets under way.

LaVell Edwards

THE AUDIBLE

A quarterback comes to the line, places his hands under the center, and sees something in the defense he doesn't like. Time to call an audible. This is decision making on the fly in a moment's notice. The whole team has to watch and listen to the quarterback, and then adjust to the new plan.

Life is full of audibles—last-minute changes that you didn't expect. My mission president used to say, "Don't write your goals in stone—write them in pencil. Goals need to be adjusted at times." Ask any group of adults if their lives have turned out just the way they planned or thought they would. No one will raise a hand. You have to have a Plan B, and sometimes a Plan C and D. When David confronted Goliath, he didn't bring just one stone, he brought five. Sometimes you have to think on your feet. When it comes to the most important decisions in life, we've been promised help "in the very hour, yea, in the very moment" about what we should do (see D&C 100:6). When life gives you the unexpected, be prepared to "audible."

Trying to maintain order during a legalized gang brawl involving 80 toughs with a little whistle, a hanky, and a ton of prayer.

A REFEREE, EXPLAINING HIS JOB

HEARING FOOTSTEPS

You're a receiver—you run a curl pattern, turn, and, as you go up for the ball, you hear the defensive back coming from behind. He's huffing and puffing and closing fast. What do you do? Tense up? Pull your arms in close and brace for impact? No. Just *catch the ball.*

Coaches often tell players, "You know you're going to get hit, right? You'll get hit whether or not you catch the ball, so you might as well catch it."

In life, good things happen, and bad things happen. You're going to get hit, period. So you might as well catch the ball. Do the right thing even when the hit is coming—just catch the ball—and let the consequence follow.

SOMETHING TO PROVE

Watch out for a team with something to prove, or a team with a "chip on its shoulder." If I were a coach, I wouldn't mind if the media overlooked my school. I'd rather be underrated than overrated in the eyes of others. Rudy Ruettiger, the main character of the classic football movie *Rudy*, observed, "Players always complain when the newspapers write about how badly they're doing. But coaches love it. Players who are mad at the media are players with something to prove." Like Rudy, many NCAA players were told they would never make it to the college level. They are often grateful for that advice, because it gave them unbounded motivation to prove the critics wrong.

Similarly, we can live our lives with "something to prove." We've all had our critics—teachers, peers, or old girlfriends who didn't think we'd amount to much. What a gift! Now we have something to prove. To paraphrase the scripture, "Satan desires to have us that he may sift us as wheat." He'll often tell us, "You'll never make it, you're just not celestial material." This gives us something to prove. This life is the place to do the proving. "And we will prove them herewith, to see if they will do all things what-soever the Lord their God shall command them" (Abraham 3:25).

You may not realize it at the time, but a kick in the teeth may be the best thing in the world for you.

Walt Disney

When I was the last man on the depth chart at Notre Dame, I didn't need the coaches to make me mad. Every day I went out to practice and was a human tackling dummy. Getting beat to a pulp every day gave me all the anger I needed to resolve to figure out a way not to let it happen again. There was no other way. If I had sat back and taken it, I wouldn't have lasted a week. Those monsters would have broken me into a million pieces. As it was, they beat me up badly. That was their job. But I didn't have to take it with a smile. And I didn't. Getting mad made me think of ways to beat those guys. It gave me the strength and determination to fight back.

RUDY RUETTIGER

ELDER DAVID B. HAIGHT

106 to 6

When I tell you that I played football in high school, it is not a boast. It is more of a confession.

You see, football came to our country town later than most. The school board had neither the money for equipment nor for a coach. Instead, we all played basketball. The only equipment you needed was a pair of shoes.

Finally, our principal saved enough to buy 12 inexpensive football outfits, not including shoes. The cleated shoes were too expensive, so we used our basketball shoes instead. Our coach was recruited from the faculty. He was selected because he had once watched a football game. We learned a few simple plays. We learned how to tackle—or so we thought. Then we set off for our first game with Twin Falls, the previous year's Idaho state champions.

We dressed and went out to the field to warm up. Their team's school band started to play. They had more students in the band than we had in our entire high school! Then through the gates came their team. Our team of 12—a full team of 11 plus one all-around substitute—watched in amazement as they kept coming through the gates, all 39 of them in full uniform.

The game was most interesting. To say it was a learning experience is rather mild. After two plays we didn't have any desire to have the ball, so we would kick it away, and soon they would score. Our main problem was how to get rid of the ball. It was less punishing for us when we weren't being tackled!

In the final minutes of the game the other team became a little reckless. A wild pass fell into the arms of Clifford Lee, who was playing halfback with me. He was startled. He didn't know what to do until he saw [the entire opposing team] thundering after him. Then he knew what to do! He was not interested in six points. He ran for his life.

He was fast. He made a touchdown, and we finally got six points on the board. We really didn't deserve the six points, but with our torn shirts and socks and our bloody shins, we took them anyway. The final score: 106 to 6!

ELDER DAVID B. HAIGHT

66 That game was definitely a learning experience. It taught me that a team (or an individual) must be prepared. Success in all things depends on preparation. 99

ELDER DAVID B. HAIGHT

66 Did I win? Did I lose? Those are the wrong questions. The correct answer is: Did I make my best effort? That's what matters. The rest of it just gets in the way. In classical times, the courageous struggle for a noble cause was considered success in itself. Sadly, that ideal has been forgotten. But it is well worth remembering. 99

JOHN WOODEN

"WINNING ISN'T EVERYTHING— IT'S THE ONLY THING!"

This statement has been widely attributed to legendary Green Bay Packer coach Vince Lombardi. Vince Lombardi probably heard it from UCLA coach Henry Russell Sanders. In later years, Lombardi claimed that what he really said was, "Winning isn't everything, the will to win is the only thing."

Personally, I prefer the philosophy of legendary UCLA basketball coach John Wooden, who felt that winning, like so many other things in sports, is something you really have no control over. The only thing you have control over is how you play—not how the other team plays. To give it your best, to "leave it all out there on the field," is the definition of success.

The greatest disappointments in sports are not from losing, but from losing when you could have won but you were careless—you made stupid mistakes, you weren't prepared, or you didn't play your best.

I'D LIKE TO THANK MY O-LINE

It was the closing seconds of the 2006 UNLV at BYU game. BYU had the game well in hand, so the second-string offense was on the field, doing running plays into the line to run out the clock. Running back Mike Hague took the handoff and ran right into the pile. Suddenly, the most unexpected thing happened. The pile was stuck. So he twisted out of the pile and sprinted 87 yards down the sideline for a touchdown.

After the game, the media asked Mike how it felt. Do you know what he did? He thanked the offensive line! "What?" I thought. "They were all in a pile. You did a 360 and left them all behind!" But Mike Hague was smart. Football is a team sport, and he thanked the O-line anyway.

Think back to your greatest accomplishments. Did you do them all by yourself? Chances are, there have been people blocking for you all your life: moms, dads, leaders, teachers, and coaches, often going without recognition, who helped you get where you are today. Not everyone gets to be a collegiate athlete— even more uncommon is one who shows genuine gratitude.

I guarantee you . . . you are going to come across another player in life's game of football that is bigger and tougher than you. Whether it's immorality, or alcohol, or peer pressure, or stress, or jealousy, or whatever it is, something is going to come across your path that you cannot beat on your own . . . get ahold of the other players on your team. You've got some tough players blocking for you, your bishops, your stake presidents. . . . These bishops and these stake presidents and these parents are not on the other team, they're on *your* team. They're going to block for you. And if you're having a tough play that you cannot take, then it's time to call them in and say, "Man, you gotta block for me!" If you have a friend that's getting beat up and thrown into the ground by Satan . . . block for 'em!

TROY DUNN

> "Baseball players are smarter than football players. How often do you see a baseball team penalized for too many men on the field?"

JIM BOUTON

> "The players on the Maryland football team all made straight As. Their Bs were a little crooked."

JOHNNY WALKER

"College football is a sport that bears
the same relation to education that
bullfighting does to agriculture."

ELBERT HUBBARD

> **❝** You have to play this game like somebody just hit your mother with a two-by-four. **❞**

DAN BIRDWELL

> **❝** We can't run. We can't pass. We can't stop the run. We can't stop the pass. We can't kick. Other than that, we're just not a very good football team right now. **❞**

BRUCE COSLET
on the Bengals' 1997 season

66 Thanksgiving dinners take eighteen hours to prepare. They are consumed in twelve minutes. Halftimes take twelve minutes. This is not coincidence. 99

ERMA BOMBECK

66 I have seen women walk right past a TV set with a football game on and—this always amazes me—not stop to watch, even if the TV is showing replays of what we call a 'good hit,' which is a tackle that causes at least one major internal organ to actually fly out of a player's body. 99

DAVE BARRY

STEVE YOUNG

FROM STARDOM TO...
BACKUP?

Steve Young had a stellar college career and signed a huge contract with the startup United States Football League (USFL). Eventually, the USFL fizzled, and Steve Young found himself in the NFL playing backup to Joe Montana. For three years, he watched from the sidelines as Joe Montana moved the San Francisco 49ers offense down the field.

Finally, after waiting and learning, Steve got his chance, and he led the 49ers to the top. Not only did they win the Super Bowl, but Steve Young was named the Super Bowl XXIX MVP, and in 2005 was inducted into the Pro Football Hall of Fame. It would be easy to center your life and your self-worth around that career, wouldn't it?

I've been able to put everything in perspective the last couple of years. Now when something comes in and hits me, it doesn't go all the way to the center. I think that's because my life is not centered on what others think of me. I have something else at the center of my life. Don't waste your time worshiping sports heroes, rock stars, movie idols, or CEOs. Please, just worship God, your Heavenly Father.

STEVE YOUNG

A FEW THINGS NOT TO LEARN FROM SPORTS. . .

So, sports are the perfect metaphor for life, right? Well, not really. Before we finish up, we'd better make it clear—there are a number of things *not* to learn from sports. Combine massive media attention, enormous salaries, and the worship of millions of fans, and you have a perfect recipe for pride.

I'm old enough to have witnessed an NBA strike, an MLB strike, and an NFL strike. These were always a big turnoff for fans, since most people earn a fraction of what pro athletes earn. Those hit the hardest during these strikes were those who took tickets, ran concessions, or swept floors at the arena. During a pro basket-ball strike back in 1998, NBA players attempted to hold a "charity game" for some of the lower-paid athletes in their ranks because "some of their players were only making a quarter of a million dollars a year and were having a hard time making ends meet."

During the last several years, as our world has become more unstable, it has become easier to identify what real heroes are—warriors who put their lives on the line for others, like firefighters, law enforcement officers, parents, and those who serve in our military. "Sports warriors," those who have developed great athletic talent and supply the public with great entertainment, are exciting to watch, but they're another category. My hero? My dad, hands down.

Some believe that sports build character.
I believe that sports reveal character. I see too many players
who are characters today. I like a player with character.

JOHN WOODEN

NFL =
NOT FOR LONG . . .

The average athlete in the National Football League is employed there for only three to four years—in other words, "not for long." If you're a young person who believes you can skip English, math, and science because you're going to make it big in sports, be careful. Be sure you get an education in between your winning seasons—you will need it.

Sportswriter Rick Reilly observed, "Filing for bankruptcy is a long-standing tradition for NBA players, 60% of whom, according to the *Toronto Star,* are broke five years after they retire." Reilly continued, "The other 40% deliver the *Toronto Star.*"

As with any victory in life, it won't last for long. Success is not a destination, it's a journey—meaning you can never say, "I've arrived." In sports, the game is over after four quarters—that's why it's called a "game." In life, the contest is one day at a time, with no end in sight. There will always be new defeats to learn from, new opponents to conquer, new challenges to overcome.

FAN BEHAVIOR

I love the definition of a "fan" on Wikipedia:

> Fans of a particular thing or person constitute its fanbase or fandom. They often show their enthusiasm by starting a fan club, holding fan conventions, creating fanzines, writing fan mail, or promoting the object of their interest and attention. In a few cases, individual fans may become so fascinated with the objects of their infatuation that they become obsessive.

Some say the word *fan* comes from the word *fanatic*. Others say it developed from having an interest in, or a "fancy" for, a team. Whatever the origin, some make it part of their personal identity, and it becomes a matter of the utmost importance to them, as if there's some kind of virtue in being a fan. I've even heard fans chastise other fans for not being fan enough. "You're not a real fan," they say.

Okay, now it's true confession time—are you a fan? Have you ever become emotionally involved with a team to the point that you: Pace during the game? Yell at the television? Lose sleep if your team loses?

Me too. But I'm working on it. On the following pages are a few ideas that help keep me grounded.

> **&&**We are inclined that if we watch a football game or baseball game, we have taken part in it. **99**

PRESIDENT JOHN F. KENNEDY

> **&&**I decry the great waste of time that people put into watching inane television. I am not antisports. I enjoy watching a good football game or a good basketball game. But I see so many men who become absolutely obsessed with sports. I believe their lives would be enriched if, instead of sitting on the sofa and watching a game that will be forgotten tomorrow, they would read and think and ponder. **99**

PRESIDENT GORDON B. HINCKLEY

VICARIOUS HEROISM

I read an article in high school called "The Vicarious Heroism of the Sports Spectator" by Michael Roberts. Vicarious Heroism: What in the world is that? Is it possible to be a hero yourself, because someone else succeeded on the court, field or gridiron? Of course not, we would say. I don't believe in vicarious heroism, and neither does anyone I know. At least not consciously. Vicarious heroism says that when "my" team succeeds, then somehow I am a hero. I'm a champion by proxy.

Professional teams tie themselves to a state, or a city—and this is not an accident—it's savvy marketing. When the Philadelphia Flyers won the NHL championship in the 1970s, Time magazine proclaimed, "Philadelphia is at long last a winner." Michael Roberts commented, "what was tangible, precisely speaking, was the Stanley Cup, a large hideous piece of metalwork worth less than $100, which came into possession of the Flyers' management for a year. . . .What had Philadelphia—the civic entity—won? That's an elusive, metaphysical question. But for sure millions of residents were being counseled to think more highly of themselves for the Flyers' accomplishments."

If . . . our attitude towards life depends upon the praise of men, the level of interest rates, the outcome of a particular election or athletic contest—we are too much at the mercy of men and circumstance.

ELDER NEAL A. MAXWELL

BRAGGING RIGHTS

Another evidence of the strange phenomenon of vicarious heroism is the notion of "bragging rights." After the next big rivalry game, go to the fan blogs, or listen to sports radio. Notice the boasting, the taunting, the bragging, the trash-talking, not from players on the team, mind you, but from the fans. From spectators who only watched the contest from a distance!

Some will say, "Hey, it ain't bragging if you can do it." But that's just the point. I didn't do it, and neither did anyone else in the stands. We're just fans. When I go to work or priesthood meeting do I have the "right" to taunt the others who chose another team to root for, or who chose a different institution of higher learning? Sure, some good-natured teasing is no big deal, but sometimes it goes over the top.

Although I consider myself a sports fan, this philosophy has helped me to keep it in perspective: I'm not going to brag about the accomplishments of others (since I have no right to), and I'm not going to be bothered by the vicarious bragging of other fans when "my" team loses.

To brag little—to show well—to crow gently, if in luck— to pay up, to own up, and to shut up, if beaten, are the virtues of a sporting man.

OLIVER WENDELL HOLMES

> **❝** Like every other instrument man has invented, sport can be used for good and evil purposes. Used badly, it can encourage personal vanity, greedy desire for victory and even hatred for rivals, an intolerant esprit de corps and contempt for people who are beyond an arbitrary selected pale. **❞**

ALDOUS HUXLEY

> **❝** Sportsmanship is the spirituality in athletics, and we believe that the Church athletic program is a spiritual program. If it wasn't we wouldn't continue it, because our purpose is to build men and women of character and spirituality. **❞**

PRESIDENT EZRA TAFT BENSON

BE TRUE TO YOUR SCHOOL

But didn't the Beach Boys teach us to "be true to your school"? Is there anything wrong with cheering for "your" team? Boy, I sure hope not, because I love fall afternoons at the football stadium.

Like with everything else in life, we just don't want to get out of balance. Some sports fans spend time on their team blog every day, they read every article, they watch every report, and *nothing* gets in the way of game day. They're elated if their team wins, and depressed all weekend if they lose. Here's the question I ask myself if I think I'm getting lopsided: *"What would happen if I devoted the same level of energy and passion to accomplishing my own goals as I do to watching others reach for theirs?"*

The coach whose philosophy I have admired as much as any coach I've ever been associated with is Amos Alonzo Stagg. He was coaching football at the University of Chicago when they were a national power. After one very successful year a reporter said, "Coach Stagg, it was a great year! A really great year." Coach Stagg said, "I won't know for another twenty years or so whether you're correct." He meant that it would take that long to see how the youngsters under his supervision turned out in life. That's how I feel. I'm most proud of the athlete who does well with his life. That's where success is. Basketball is just a very small part of it.

JOHN WOODEN

66 After intensive study and contemplation, I have reached this conclusion: "YOU CAN'T GET OUT OF LIFE ALIVE!" So why not enjoy it to the utmost? You can die in the bleachers or you can die on the field, so you might as well get out on the field of life and have a good time! Enjoy the grand adventure. Make it the most positively charged experience possible. **99**

LES BROWN

POST-GAME

George F. Will remarked, "Sports serve society by providing vivid examples of excellence." I agree. I love sports because I love to see athletes stretch and strive and compete. I love to watch instant replays, and I often shake my head and ask, "How did he do that?" The excellence of these athletes on the court, field, and gridiron compels me to strive for excellence in my personal pursuits, because one day, our entire lives will be on "instant replay," and we'll account for what we did with our time in this "contest" called earth life.

One college football team had this motto:

"Anyone, Anytime, Anywhere. Leave No Doubt."

This team wanted to announce to the world that they would play any team, on any date, at any location, and then they would leave no doubt as to their competitive will.

For Latter-day Saints, we've been asked to do something very similar—to stand as witnesses of God at all times and in all things and in all places. In other words, we will show our faith to anyone, anytime, and anywhere—and we will leave no doubt as to what we believe.

SOURCES

p. v. Joe Paterno. http://www.foxnews.com/story/0,2933,441245,00.html

p. vii. Spencer W. Kimball. *The Teachings of Spencer W. Kimball,* edited by Edward L. Kimball (Bookcraft, 1982), 290.

p. 13. James Naismith. http://www.xquotes.net/author/James _Naismith.html.

p. 14. J. Reuben Clark, Jr. "Aaronic Priesthood," *Improvement Era,* February 1936, 108.

pp. 21–23. Thomas S. Monson, "The Call for Courage," *Ensign,* May 2004, 54.

pp. 25–26. Sheri Dew story. *No One Can Take Your Place* (Deseret Book, 2004), 196–98.

p. 28. John Wooden. Coach John Wooden with Steve Jamison, *Wooden: A Lifetime of Observations and Reflections On and Off the Court* (Contemporary Books, 1997), 54.

p. 35. Mike Maxwell story. See Lee Benson, *Deseret News,* August 12, 1980.

p. 37. Rick Pitino, *Success Is a Choice* (Broadway Books, 1997), 2.

p. 38. Spencer W. Kimball. Edward L. Kimball and Andrew E. Kimball, *Spencer W. Kimball* (Bookcraft, 1977), 65–66.

p. 49. Howard W. Hunter. *The Teachings of Howard W. Hunter,* edited by Clyde J. Williams (Bookcraft, 1997), 63.

p. 58. Luke Salisbury. In *The Gigantic Book of Baseball Quotations* (Skyhorse Publishing, 2007), 633.

pp. 60–61. Thomas S. Monson. "Do Your Duty—That Is Best," *Ensign,* November 2005, 56.

pp. 64, 67. Dale Murphy, *Latter-day Legends: Self-Esteem for Youth Fireside* (KBYU- TV/Forever Young Foundation, 1996), videotape in possession of the author.

p. 73. Ezra Taft Benson. *The Teachings of Ezra Taft Benson* (Bookcraft, 1988), 437.

p. 77. Hank Aaron. In *Gigantic Book of Baseball Quotations,* 204.

p. 81. Paul Richards. In *Gigantic Book of Baseball Quotations,* 26.

p. 82. Harmon Killebrew. In Paul H. Dunn, *Win if You Will* (Bookcraft, 1972), 133.

p. 85. Bill Veeck, Deion Sanders, and Earl Weaver. In *Gigantic Book of Baseball Quotations,* 626, 606, 616.

p. 87. Wally Joyner. In Shellie M. Frey, *Winning Spirit* (Brigham Young University Press, 1996), 45. Ron Fairly. In *Gigantic Book of Baseball Quotations,* 160.

p. 88. Nolan Ryan. In Steve Riach, *Life Lessons from Baseball* (Honor Books, 2004), 7.

p. 90. Mark Twain. In *Gigantic Book of Baseball Quotations,* 625.

p. 92. Bill Veeck, Roger Kahn, and Harry Truman. In *Gigantic Book of Baseball Quotations,* 619, 621, 650.

p. 94. Mark Beltaire. In *Gigantic Book of Baseball Quotations,* 645.

p. 99. George Carlin. *Brain Droppings* (Hyperion, 1997), 52–53.

p. 102. Frank Gifford. http://quotations-book.com/quote/15436/. George F. Will. http://www.quotes-zone.com/quotes/29/violence.php.

p. 104. LaVell Edwards. In *Tradition, Spirit, Honor,* DVD presentation (Deseret Book, 2007). Bronco Mendenhall. "The Bronco Way," *BYU Magazine,* Winter 2007, 26.

p. 111. Herschel Walker. http://quotationsbook.com/author/7484/.

p. 114. LaVell Edwards. *LaVell: Airing It Out* (Shadow Mountain, 1995), 81.

p. 123. Rudy Ruettiger. *Rudy's Insights for Winning in Life* (Rudy International Publications, 1999), 36.

p. 124. Walt Disney. http://www.brainyquote.com/quotes/authors/w/walt_disney.html.

p. 127. Rudy Ruettiger. *Rudy's Insights for Winning in Life,* 39.

pp. 129–31. David B. Haight. "The Message: You Are Needed," *New Era,* May 1991, 4.

p. 132. David B. Haight. "The Message: You Are Needed," 4. John Wooden. *Wooden: A Lifetime of Observations,* 56.

p. 139. Troy Dunn. *Life Is a Football Game,* talk on cassette (Covenant Recordings, 1991).

p. 140. Jim Bouton. http://en.thinkexist.com/quotes/Jim_Bouton/. Johnny Walker. http://www.creativequotations.com/tqs/tq-football.htm.

p. 142. Elbert Hubbard. http://www.yourdictionary.com/bullfighting.

p. 145. Dan Birdwell. http://www.denny-davis.net/poemfiles/ftball.htm. Bruce Cosley. http://www.10ktruth.com/the_quotes/football.htm.

p. 146. Erma Bombeck. http://www.goodreads.com/quotes/show/17695. Dave Barry. http://www.quotegarden.com/football.html.

p. 150. Steve Young. *The Best of Personal Excellence* (Executive Excellence Publishing, 1997), 52.

p. 156. John Wooden. *Wooden: A Lifetime of Observations,* 93.

p. 158. Rick Reilly. http://sports.espn.go.com/espnmag/story?id=3469271.

p. 163. John F. Kennedy. http://www.quotegarden.com/sports.html. Gordon B. Hinckley. "First Presidency Message: Life's Obligations," *Ensign,* February 1999, 2.

pp. 165–66. Michael Roberts, "The Vicarious Heroism of the Sports Spectator," *The New Republic,* November 23, 1974, 17–20.

p. 167. Neal A. Maxwell. " 'Be of Good Cheer,'" *Ensign,* November 1982, 66.

p. 169. Oliver Wendell Holmes. http://www.famousquotes.com/show.php?_id=1028783.

p. 171. Aldous Huxley. http://www.hin-duonnet.com/2002/11/14/stories/2002111407012100.htm. Ezra Taft Benson. *Teachings of Ezra Taft Benson,* 437.

p. 174. John Wooden. *Wooden: A Lifetime of Observations,* 105.

p. 176. Les Brown. *Live Your Dreams* (William Morrow and Co., 1992), 193.

p. 179. George Will. http://www.quotes.net/quote/6602.